Boredom BUSTERS for Dogs
40 Tail-Wagging Games and Adventures

By Nikki Moustaki

D1254611

A Division of BowTie, Inc.
Irvine, CA

Vice President, Chief Content Officer: June Kikuchi
Vice President, Kennel Club Books: Andrew DePrisco
Production Supervisor: Jessica Jaensch
Production Coordinator: Tracy Burns
Art Director: Cindy Kassebaum
BowTie Press: Jennifer Calvert, Amy Deputato, Lindsay Hanks,
Karen Julian, Elizabeth L. McCaughey, Roger Sipe, Jarelle S. Stein

Illustrations courtesy of/reproduced with permission of: **Seth Casteel**—front cover, 56;
Judith Wolfe—4; **Tara Darling**—10, 12, 27, 30, 33, 48, 52; **Gina Cioli and Pamela Hunnicutt/
BowTie Inc.**—15; **Shutterstock® Images**—all other images

Library of Congress Cataloging-in-Publication Data

Moustaki, Nikki 1970-
  Boredom busters for dogs : 40 tail-wagging games and adventures / by Nikki Moustaki.
      p. cm.
  Includes bibliographical references and index
      ISBN 978-1-935484-17-2 (alk. paper)
      1. Dogs—Behavior 2. Dogs—Training 3. Human-animal relationships I. Title
      SF 433.M678 2010
      636.7'0887—dc22

                              2009041671

BowTie Press®
A Division of BowTie, Inc.   Printed and bound in China
3 Burroughs   14 13 12 11 10   3 4 5 6 7 8 9 10
Irvine, California 92618

Table of CONTENTS

WHEN CAPTIVE POLAR BEAR Gus began exhibiting obsessive-compulsive behaviors, zookeepers were told he needed something to do. Like Gus, a bored, anxious, or stressed domestic dog requires enriching activities to keep him healthy and happy.

Enriching Your
DOG'S LIFE

In the mid-1990s, zookeepers at the Central Park Zoo in New York City noticed that their 700-pound male polar bear, Gus, seemed to be coming unhinged. Gus swam back and forth in his small pool day after day, for hours on end, in continuous figure eights. It was obvious to both zoo visitors and zookeepers that something was desperately wrong with the bear. Not knowing how to respond to Gus's apparent unhappiness, the zoo hired an animal behaviorist to study Gus and try to resolve his problems.

The verdict? Years of life in captivity had turned the poor bear neurotic, which had led him to exhibit obsessive and compulsive behaviors, probably to prevent himself from going out of his fluffy polar bear mind. Quite simply, Gus was in desperate need of something interesting to do.

The animal behaviorist recommended that the zoo implement enrichment activities for Gus and enhance his environment in ways that would stimulate some of his natural tendencies and break his neurotic patterns. Zookeepers installed a polar-bear-entertaining whirlpool and gave Gus interactive toys. They started offering him food in packages he had to open, hid other food around the habitat for him to track down, and froze fish in giant blocks of ice for him to break into. Gus appeared to be thrilled with the new additions to his home and daily life. He stopped his neurotic swimming pattern as he learned to play and forage as he would have in the wild. This is what pet enrichment is all about: keeping an animal active and engaged in his environment by offering him activities to stimulate natural behaviors.

As Gus so aptly demonstrated, lack of enrichment can cause stress, anxiety, and boredom, leading to problems. In your dog, they can include such behaviors as inappropriate elimination, excessive barking, and furniture dismantlement. It's a recipe for dogsaster that can end with a trip to the local shelter or a classified ad: Take my puppy, please!

Many of these problems can be solved by adding enriching activities to your dog's life. This book explores some simple ways to provide your dog with stimulating environmental enrichment to keep him happy, healthy, and out of trouble. If enrichment can work for a bored polar bear in the Central Park Zoo, it can certainly work for the bored or anxious dog in your home.

Daily Activities
AND TYPES OF ENRICHMENT

Dogs are fans of routine. Wanting to know what to expect is natural for canines. Both wild dogs and wolves are pack animals, and a pack will engage in similar activities daily, although its behaviors and patterns can change based on the time of year (for example, when it's breeding season and there are pups needing care). Like his wild counterparts, your dog does best when occupied with activities that are a part of a routine. But there is one big difference between the wild dog and the house dog—the latter is not in charge of his own life.

Without prey to hunt, a canine pack to interact with, and the daily struggle for survival, your dog must rely on his human pack for order and activity. Most dogs, after all, were originally bred to work. If you don't enrich a dog's environment, his work may be to dismantle stuff. You didn't need those Victorian chairs, did you?

Although your dog likes routine, he also needs variety to keep him interested. There are four types of enrichment activities—solo, social, environmental, and variance; your dog will do best when you engage him in all of them.

Solo: Solo activities encourage a dog to engage in an activity alone. Because it's critical for him to learn to play by himself, happily and safely, you need to learn what motivates your dog so you can choose the solo activities he will find most rewarding and fun. Solo enrichment

offers your dog something positive to do in your absence (or when you are doing something else), such as playing with interesting and challenging toys and hunting down his food.

Social: Social enrichment involves interactions between your dog and you, with other people, and with other dogs. Social enrichment for your dog includes activities such as engaging in a game of tug-of-war with you and enjoying playdates with canine friends.

Environmental: Enriching your dog's environment to give him activity options will save your home, garden, and sanity. This enrichment may include giving your pooch his own space in which to play, including such amenities as a digging pit and a wading pool.

Variance: Dogs love new smells and new areas to explore. Opportunities to add variance

to your dog's life include taking him on different routes during your walks and traveling to new places. You can also add variety by teaching your dog new behaviors or tricks or getting him involved in canine sports.

Finding Your
DOG'S MOTIVATION

Understanding your dog's breed can help you determine what kinds of activities may most captivate your companion and work best to enrich his life. Below are some of the common characteristics found in various breeds; because there are more than 400 individual breeds, we'll look at them in the American Kennel Club's seven breed groups. They include the Herding Group (*left*), the Hound Group, the Non-Sporting Group, the Sporting Group, the Terrier Group, the Toy Group, and the Working Group.

Herding Group: Dogs in the Herding Group—including the Australian Shepherd, the Border Collie, and the Pembroke Welsh Corgi—are generally very active and intelligent and need a lot of enrichment activities to keep them entertained and physically and emotionally healthy. Herding breeds tend to excel at agility and other canine sports. A bored herding dog can become destructive and bossy—trying to herd his owner and other members of the family.

Hound Group: Members of the Hound Group will either be scenthounds such as the Bloodhound and the Beagle, single-mindedly tracking down intriguing smells, or sighthounds, such as the Greyhound and the Afghan Hound, determinedly pursuing almost anything that moves. The gastronomically enthusiastic scenthounds (also known as chowhounds) will enjoy hide-and-seek food games. The born-to-chase sighthounds will readily take to sports such as flyball and lure coursing. A bored hound may become a barking or howling neighborhood nuisance, or he could become lazy and overweight.

Dogs who belong to the Working Group, such as the Boxer, are happiest when they are active in mind and in body.

Non-Sporting Group: Non-sporting breeds, such as the Dalmatian, the Chinese Shar-Pei, and the French Bulldog, have been grouped together not because they are similar to each other but because they fall into the same category—companion dogs who no longer perform their original functions. Read up on your particular breed to discover what may best motivate your dog.

Sporting Group: Among the various breeds composing this group are pointers, retrievers, and spaniels. Any dog with *retriever* in his breed name is going to be an active, social dog who likes fetching games and probably revels in being in the water. Spaniels and pointers love to be outside finding new scents and enjoy taking part in social games. Left

without something to do, these dogs may become destructive kitchen-counter surfers and trash divers.

Terrier Group: Dogs in the Terrier Group, among them the Bull, Parson Russell, and Norfolk Terriers, will likely be into digging, chasing small objects, and removing the squeakers from toys. After all, they were bred to ferret out and destroy prey. Many breeds in this group have seemingly boundless energy and appreciate social activities. A bored terrier will find his own activities, including digging up the carpet and trying to eat other household pets (or at least chasing them about and attempting to nibble on them!).

Toy Group: Toy breeds, classified for their diminutive size and role as companions rather than their similarity to each other, actually share characteristics with breeds in other groups. For example, the Yorkshire and Silky Terriers are as tenacious as any official breed in the Terrier Group. Research your dog's breed to find common characteristics and activities he may enjoy.

Working Group: Working dogs were all bred for specific jobs. Whether they are protecting a flock of sheep, pulling a sled, or retrieving items from the water, these dogs want to feel useful. Dogs who belong to the Working Group, such as the Boxer, the Portuguese Water Dog, and the Siberian Husky, are happiest when they are active in mind and in body. Activities these dogs may enjoy include jogging, carting (pulling loads), and tracking.

Toy breeds, such as this Chihuahua, not only make great companions but also are good candidates for a variety of enrichment activities.

The Mutt Group

No, there isn't really a mutt group, but your Heinz 57 dog probably has one or more recognizable breeds in him. Use your best guess or get a DNA test to figure out your dog's particular parentage, and tailor your enrichment activities accordingly. For example, a Lab/German Shepherd mix might like retrieving games and obedience training. A Greyhound/Golden Retriever mix might like prey-driven games with both chasing and fetching elements.

By studying information about your dog's breed, you may learn what's likely to inspire him, but you will still need to observe your dog to learn exactly what motivates him. When you find out what enrichment activities he favors, make them a regular part of his day. Be consistent—he will notice when you skip a regular activity, and he will show you that he's bored. That's why it's good to have a variety of activities he can engage in as well as multiple toys to play with in case an enrichment emergency, such as bad weather, disrupts your regular routine.

Solo
ENRICHMENT

Unless you have a doggy cam, you're probably not completely sure what your dog is doing while you're away. The evidence of his activities only becomes clear when you come home to find the trash can upside-down, the carpet in a new polka-dot pattern (brown is in, isn't it?), and the walls looking like the guys from *Extreme Makeover: Home Edition* broke in while you were away (you needed to replace the drywall anyway, didn't you?). Here are some activities to help safely occupy your dog while he's flying solo as well as ways to make mealtimes more exciting.

Food for Fun

Given a choice between a ride in the car and a T-bone steak, most dogs will meet you at the barbecue grill rather than the garage. Using food to keep a dog entertained can turn a holy terror into a holy terrier—complete with halo and angel's wings.

Hunting for Food

One daily activity most domesticated dogs miss is the hunt for food. Handing a hunter a dish of food is almost insulting, and it's definitely boring. A dog in the wild can spend hours every day looking for food. A domestic dog spends just a few minutes on his most important daily activity. So why not make eating a little more interesting and interactive? Here are some ways to turn food into a happy distraction.

Hide-and-seek courses: For each meal, portion your dog's food into small containers, and hide them all over the house. However, make sure to show your dog what you're doing the first few times so he gets the idea he has to look for them. Once your dog understands that he has to search for his food, you can place the containers in different areas each day to make a more challenging hunt. This is also great for dogs who seem to inhale their food—eating slowly is healthier and safer.

Kibble scatter: Instead of pouring your dog's dry food into a bowl, scatter it in a place in the yard where your dog doesn't do his business and where you don't use harmful chemicals or in a room where you don't mind having the floor a bit less than clean for a while. If your dog's regular meal doesn't include kibble, use small amounts of weight-control kibble, sliced

This dog is on the hunt for some tasty treats. Make meals more challenging by hiding or scattering kibble for your pet to find.

carrots, or apple chunks (no peels) as a treat. If you use food or treats in addition to your dog's daily meals, keep his calorie count in mind.

Sneaky snacks: As with your dog's regular meal, you can hide his snacks all over the house and make him search for them. This is a particularly good trick to use just before you leave the house, especially if you have a nervous dog suffering from separation anxiety. It will distract your dog from your departure and give him something to do while you're gone. Make sure to lead him to the snacks the first few times you do this to make sure that he understands the game.

Working for Food

Another way to enrich your dog's feeding experience and ensure that life is more interesting for him is to make him work, not just hunt, for his food.

Food-dispensing toys: One of the most ingenious products to hit pet store shelves in the past few years is the food-dispensing toy. This type of toy comes in many shapes (such as cones, balls, bottles, and bones) and in many materials (such as pliable rubber and hard plastic). If you have a puppy, an active dog, or a dog who suffers from separation anxiety, you absolutely need several of these toys on hand. You can even set aside part of your dog's regular food allotment to disperse among a few of these toys. Having several also allows you to wash some while the others are in use. Make sure that the toys you choose are very durable.

To make the activity more interesting still, place a high-value food at the bottom of one of the toys, such as a piece of frankfurter, a dollop of peanut butter, or a cube of cheese (something your

Chomping on Chewies

Dogs love to chew, especially young dogs. Chewable treats, or "chewies," include rawhide, pig's ears and snouts, cow hooves, bully sticks, and sterilized bones (from the pet store)—anything that encourages your dog to chew on something other than your shoes. Chewing helps teething puppies relieve some of their gum pain and helps keep teeth clean. Always supervise your dog with chew toys and replace them when they get small, slimy, and dirty. Some chewies are edible, and others are not. Beware of synthetic, inedible chew toys—some of these have been said to create serious gastrointestinal issues if the dog consumes them.

dog goes nuts for), and then put his regular dry food on top. Now partially plug the top of the toy with a dog treat, such as a strip of dried chicken or beef. Your dog will have to work to get the plug out, remove the kibble, and spend some time trying to get at the high-value food at the bottom.

Another option is to spread peanut butter inside the toy, add some wet canned food, stuff the rest with kibble, and then freeze the toy—this is particularly effective with a hard rubber toy or sterilized hollow bone.

Food tear-aways: Save up some paper towel and toilet paper rolls, and fill them with kibble. Pinch and roll the ends of the roll, or plug them up with a treat that's tough to remove. Your dog will have to tear the roll to get the food. You can also use cardboard boxes and envelopes—a great way to recycle all of that junk mail you get—just make sure that your dog isn't actually consuming the paper. This activity is inexpensive and easy to set up.

You can also put kibble or treats into empty milk cartons and plastic soda bottles. Be sure to remove all plastic caps and rings before giving them to your dog and take away the bottles when they get torn or mangled. Always supervise this kind of homemade toy to ensure that your dog is not consuming the cardboard or plastic. Most dogs can tell the difference between the kibble and a tasteless carton, but it's best to be on the safe side.

Hot dog dive and bob: If you have a dog who loves water, such as a retriever, toss some hot dog slices into a wading pool or a large plastic container, such as a plastic storage bin, fill it with water, and then let your dog bob for the dogs. If you don't want to use hot dogs, try

Chewing and licking, a pup digs for every tasty morsel in his toy. Food-stuffed toys keep a dog occupied long after biscuits are gone.

this with your dog's regular kibble. To ensure his safety, don't leave your dog unsupervised during water activities, and drain and clean the pool or container once they are over.

Kibble pops: If you have a yard or a patio, the "kibble pop" is a great way to distract your food-motivated dog for hours. Choose a size-appropriate container for your dog; fill it with unsalted, or low-sodium, chicken broth (you can dilute it with water); and toss in kibble and treats. Freeze the concoction until solid, remove it from the container, and serve it outside on a warm day. If you have a little dog, use a small ice cube tray; if you have a big dog, use a large ice cube tray or a small plastic container.

Puzzle toys: There are a bunch of puzzle toys on the market that make your dog use brain power to get the food out. He may have to

Peanut Butter Hunter

At no other time in the history of canines has peanut butter been such a popular flavor for dogs. Dogs are not natural peanut butter hunters (there's not a lot of the stuff in the wild), but they love it. It has the added benefit of being very sticky, which makes it a great substance to smear inside hollow bones and toys.

Toys of many shapes, materials, and sizes fill a pet store's bins. Buy a variety, and rotate them to keep your doggy's boredom at bay.

remove pieces, spin pieces, or slide pieces of the puzzle to find the treats. These puzzles can keep a dog entertained for a long time!

Lots of Toys

Once you've set about enriching the life of the average puppy or active dog, your house will probably look like you robbed a pet store. An active dog should have at least ten safe toys to play with at all times, with more toys waiting for rotation. Here are some types of toys to consider buying for your dog.

Balls: Most dogs just can't get enough of these doggie playtime musts—smooth, spiky, plush, rubber, you name it, they love it! You don't need to reach for an old tennis ball; there are all types of dog toy balls on the market made to withstand chewing (tennis balls are not). When Fido is playing alone, only let him have those toys made just for him. Be sure to always choose toys appropriately sized for your dog. As for actual tennis balls—those made for play on the tennis court—they're fine for a supervised game of fetch, but don't let your dog chew on them. There are tennis-type balls made

🐾 Keeping Toys New

Some dogs get bored seeing the same toys every day; eventually those toys become "invisible" to the dogs. To keep toys like new, only let your dog have a few of them at any one time. Every couple of days, replace two or three toys, putting the "old" ones away for a while.

specifically for dogs, which stand up better to canine teeth.

Noisy toys: Some toys play music, sing, or make animal sounds; others allow you to record your voice. These seem to capture the attention of some dogs, even to the point of obsession. You know your dog is happily enriched when you're listening to a toy play "Jingle Bells" for the thousandth time. Happy holidays! Where are those earplugs?

Plush toys: Stuffed toys are a canine toy box staple unless a dog is so destructive that a plush toy doesn't last five minutes in his jaws. But for most dogs, plush toys are a lot of fun. Always supervise your dog when he is playing with these toys, and make sure they don't have small parts, such as plastic eyes, which your pet could swallow, causing serious injuries.

Prey toys: Most dogs like to chase objects, and some, such as terriers and sighthounds, have a very strong prey drive. These dogs can be kept busy with toys that move and make noise. Some of them contain motion sensors and start to vibrate or roll when they're touched. Toys with squeakers are also considered prey toys—just make sure that if your dog rips out the squeaker, you take it away immediately so he doesn't accidentally swallow it. Supervision is key to your dog's safety with toys such as these.

A pup happily carts a soft, colorful caterpillar about the yard. Plush toys can also be fetched, cuddled, and chewed, keeping your dog content.

Social
ENRICHMENT

There's little that is more fulfilling for your dog than one-on-one time with his favorite human—you! Spending time in your presence, playing a vigorous game of tug, or cuddling on the sofa makes your dog feel safe and keeps him occupied and out of trouble. Dogs are social animals, and playing with other people and animals is also important for your dog, whether that be in the dog park, during a doggy play-date, or at home with an animal companion. In this chapter, you will find several social activities that will enrich your dog's life.

For the Two of You

Bubbles, bubbles, balls, and lasers! The possibilities for play with your puppy are endless. Here are some games the two of you can enjoy together.

Bubble chase: Dogs love bubbles as much as kids do! Be sure to buy pet-specific bubbles, which are tougher and safer than regular soap bubbles; because they don't pop as easily, even when they hit the ground, most dogs have time to catch a lot of bubbles before they're gone. That's particularly appealing because doggy bubbles are little floating spheres of yummy flavor—choose from peanut butter, bacon, and chicken bubbles.

Fetch: A rollicking game of fetch is a blast for most dogs. In general, dogs will figure out that if they bring back the ball, Frisbee, or

Obedience Training

Obedience training is a major enrichment tool simply because it gives you and your dog some one-on-one time. If the two of you participate in a training class, your dog also has time with other people and dogs. Of course, your dog doesn't have to learn extensive formal obedience—simple behaviors can be enough. At the very least, every dog should master the *come*, *sit*, *down*, and *stay* cues. If you choose to teach these yourself, buy a good training book and get started.

Keep training sessions short, around ten to fifteen minutes, and make them fun and positive. Once your dog learns the basic cues, you can move on to a few tricks!

A dog plays tug with a rope toy. Don't leave your pet alone with such a toy; if ingested, pieces can cause intestinal blockage.

stick, you will throw it again and the game will continue. Some dogs, however, do have to be taught to bring back and relinquish the object. To do this, simply trade the object for something better, such as a piece of hot dog. Eventually you won't need the bribe, and your dog will fetch for the game's sake.

Laser flash: Laser toys can be great for dogs who love to chase objects. You can use any laser pointer and flash the little red dot on the ground and walls to have your dog chase

🐾 Cuddle Time

What's more enriching than a good cuddling session? Your dog will appreciate your undivided attention for some quality pets and cuddles.

it, but watch out for his eyes. Keep these play sessions brief; after about ten minutes, give your dog a treat or a favorite toy so he doesn't become frustrated. After all, your dog will never be able to catch that laser. Be warned that some dogs may become obsessive over the laser toy. If you notice your dog digging the floor where the laser beam was (and isn't currently), looking around erratically in search of the laser, or starting to chase other lights and shadows, discontinue laser play.

Tug-of-war: Most dogs love a good game of tug-of-war, which is not only great for expending energy but also good for teeth and jaws. However, there are important rules that must be followed every time the game is played. If you do not follow these rules, you'll be teaching your dog very bad habits. Tug is a stimulating game, but it can overstimulate some dogs, so follow these guidelines:

- Be sure your dog knows the *leave it* cue. If not, ending a game of tug-of-war could be difficult. To teach the cue, give the dog something he wants, then show him an item he will want more (a high-value one, such as a smelly treat), ask him to "Leave it," and trade the first item for the better one.
- Only use a toy or other object you approve for the game; if you don't, your dog may try to play tug with things such as a shoe you're trying to put on.
- Begin by tempting your dog to take one end of the toy by wiggling it in front of him. Once he takes it, pull back and praise him as you both tug. He may play-growl and whip his head back and forth—this is acceptable.
- When you're ready to quit, stop tugging and tell your dog to "Leave it." The most important part of tug is that *you* always win the game. Always.
- Once your dog lets go of the tug toy, praise him. Then either give him a treat, and remove the toy; offer him the toy for another game; or toss the tug toy a few feet away, and let him have it.
- If your dog becomes too zealous when playing tug, and you feel teeth on your hands, quit the game immediately. Tell him to "Leave it," and put away the tug toy. Do not scold your dog; just walk away. He will learn that if he isn't gentler, you won't play.

Two puppies enjoy a game of tug-of-war in the yard. If you're too tired to tussle with your dog, invite a favorite canine pal over.

Do *not* play tug games with an aggressive dog who has a history of guarding issues. If your dog tries to snap at you or doesn't seem to understand the rules, forget about playing tug, and move on to a less-stimulating game.

Out and About with Others

It is important that your dog play with other dogs and with people other than you. By doing so, he will become better socialized, and he will have more fun!

Doggy day care: If you can't schedule playdates and the dog park isn't a part of your routine (see below), try a doggy day care to give your dog some variety in his day. Great for devoted owners whose work tears them away for more hours of the day than they would like, doggy day care will keep your dog happy, safe, and out of trouble. Day care can also help to socialize your puppy.

Dog park: Dog parks are great for social interaction. Your dog will not only find wonderful new smells to investigate in a dog park but also have the opportunity to engage with other dogs on a canine level. This is different from the level on which dogs engage with us—and this level of interaction is just as important. Your dog will also be able to interact with other humans besides you.

Meet-up group: If you have a popular breed, such as a Pug or a Poodle, you'll be able to find a social dog club or meet-up group that gets together regularly to allow the dogs to play and the humans to talk about how much they love their Schnauzers.

Playdate: Does your dog have a best canine friend? If not, perhaps he should. Playdates aren't just for kids anymore; if your dog has a particular pal he likes to interact with, schedule some time for them to be together. The key word here is *interact*. Don't bother getting two dogs together who ignore each other or, worse, try to bully each other or fight.

Animal Pals at Home

Sometimes, the surest way to enrich your dog socially is to provide him with his very own companion animal at home. Dogs are, after all, pack animals.

Canine companion: Some dogs appreciate having other dogs in the house, which provides

If your dog is well socialized and interacts regularly with other dogs on walks or in the dog park, you should be able to tell whether he's Fido friendly.

companionship and a semblance of a pack order. However, some dogs do not like to have other dogs in their spaces. Male dogs in particular, especially dominant males, won't appreciate another male dog and may bully him; they might not even accept a female dog.

Before you get your dog a friend, determine whether the new dog will be appreciated, simply tolerated, or rejected outright by your dog. If your dog is well socialized and interacts regularly with other dogs on walks or in the dog park, you should be able to tell whether he's Fido friendly. Try having some playdates with other dogs at your home to determine whether your pooch has any territorial issues.

Feline friend: Many dogs get along well with cats, and they may like having one as a housemate. However, it is best to introduce a cat and a dog when they are both at a young age. If you have an older dog who has never lived around a cat, one who might have some territorial issues, or one who has a strong prey drive, you probably shouldn't bring a new kitty into the household.

A terrier mix spends a cozy day with his feline friend. The congenial companionship of another animal can enrich your dog's life.

Environmental ENRICHMENT

Enriching your dog's environment is about providing him with areas that are for him alone and stimulate some of his natural instincts. Water dogs will enjoy the opportunity to splash about in a pool, even a shallow one; most dogs, especially terriers and Dachshunds (*left*), who were bred to ferret out prey, will go to town with a digging pit. Even your puppy's crate can be made into an intriguing cavelike environment with a few simple additions. Creating a play area from ropes and tires can also be fun.

Den: Dogs feel safest when they're in a den, such as a crate, under a table, or in a closet—anywhere with three close walls and a relatively close ceiling. Wolves and wild dogs make a den by digging a cavity into the earth with a tunnel leading to it. How about turning your dog's crate into a real den? Fashion cardboard boxes into a tunnel, and tape it to your dog's crate. Put small blankets in the tunnel and crate to give your dog the opportunity to make a comfortable nest.

Digging pit: If you've got a digger on your hands and you can't keep him out of your begonias, or your yard is starting to look like an archaeological dig site, provide him with an appropriate place to enjoy excavating. A kid's sandbox or a small homemade pit filled with clean sand (*see page 50*) should do the trick. Bury toys and treats in the sand, and show him how to dig them out. Soon he'll realize there are more goodies and more fun to be had in his own sandbox than in your garden.

Ropes and tires: Get a little bit of that nostalgic small-town feeling by hanging a clean used tire outside in the yard, not for

A curious canine investigates a tire that would be the perfect size for a backyard swing in which to hide treats.

the neighborhood kids but for your dog. Hide treats, stuffed bones, and kibble inside the tire, and show your dog how to discover the goodies. Some dogs will also love biting and hanging on the tire or will appreciate a simple rope hanging from a sturdy branch. Just don't expect a four-pound Yorkie to gnaw a tractor tire.

Wading pool: If your dog loves the water, provide him with his own wading pool. You can use a kid's wading pool or make a small pond for him (with proper filtering). Add some floating toys and hot dog slices, and you've just given your water-loving canine a ticket to H_2O heaven. For safety, always supervise your dog around water, and drain and clean the pool when he is done splashing about for the day.

🐾 Clean Sand

You can get clean sand for your dog's sandbox or digging pit at just about any large toy or home improvement store. If the sand is indicated as safe for kids, it's safe for your dog.

Atop his colorful float, this dog spends a fun-filled day in a back-yard kiddie pool. Closely supervise your dog around water.

Variance

ENRICHMENT

Variety is the spice of life, especially for your beloved pooch. While maintaining a routine, be sure to vary his enrichment activities enough to keep him from getting bored or frustrated. Some dogs love to embark on adventurous outings, whether it be going for a car cruise, enjoying a visit to a dog-friendly outdoor cafe, or frolicking on the beach. Others will enjoy turning into canine athletes, being involved in organized sports such as agility and dock jumping. Try new things to find out what makes your dog's tail wag.

Outdoor Adventures

Meeting other people and new dogs and seeing new places is great socialization—and helps tire your dog out. A tired dog is a good dog! Here are a few ideas for enriching your dog's life through a little adventure.

Cruising in the car: Ah, the feeling of the wind through fur must be exhilarating! Many dogs would jump through hoops of fire for a car ride, no matter where you're going. Even if you weren't planning to go anywhere, how about a drive around the neighborhood just to give Fido a thrill? Life's short—drive! Always keep your dog's safety in mind: a dog left to roam around the car is a serious safety hazard to himself and to you. Use his crate, or purchase a specialized dog seat belt to keep everyone safe. If you let your dog stick his head out of the window, make sure he's properly restrained and wears eye protection, such as doggy goggles!

Running errands and dining out: A lot of stores allow dogs inside these days, so include your dog when you have to run errands. Most malls allow dogs inside too, but call the store or mall ahead of time to make sure your dog will be welcome. Many cafes, restaurants, and bars with outdoor seating areas allow well-behaved dogs to join their owners at (or under) the table. Think of all the great new scents! Bring some treats along—unless you're willing to share a tiny tidbit or two off your own plate.

Walking and hiking: The simplest way to vary a dog's day is to take him on walks. Consider using a slightly different route each

Safety Gear for Cruisers

Riding in the car is a blast for most dogs, but you've got to make it safe, too. There are several companies making car safety gear for dogs, including harnesses that can be buckled into the seat belt, booster seats, and netting that goes between the dog and driver. Always restrain your dog in the car. Otherwise, he could get injured in a sudden stop or interfere with your driving and cause a serious accident. If you allow your dog to ride with his head blowing in the breeze, consider buying him doggy goggles to protect his eyes.

time so he can enjoy new scents and meet new dogs and people. If you and your dog are the adventurous, outdoorsy types, find a place to hike. If you are thinking about hiking in a state park or along a public beach, call ahead to find out whether there are any restrictions concerning dogs. Most national parks prohibit dogs on their trails. Live in a big city? Explore your nearest park as your hiking grounds.

Wading and swimming: Taking your dog to the ocean, lake, or river can be a blast for you and your pooch. We know that Labs and Poodles generally love the water, but you'd be surprised at the variety of dogs that seem like they were born to swim! Always take precautions when you and your dog take a dip. Here are some ways to keep your dog safe near the shore:

- Unless your dog is a very good swimmer, always put a life jacket on him.
- Supervise your dog every second he's in the water.
- Make sure that your dog can get out of the water safely and easily.
- Some dogs need sunscreen if they're out for more than an hour or two, particularly fair-colored or hairless dogs.
- If the water is cold, limit the time your dog is in it to prevent hypothermia. If the day is warm, make sure your dog doesn't overheat.

🐾 Dancing with the Dogs

Dancing with dogs? Yes, it's called canine freestyle. It is a dance, choreographed and performed to music (sometimes in groups), in which dog and handler wear matching costumes and compete against other dog-handler teams. This sport requires a solid human-dog bond and positive-reinforcement training. If you love to dance and your dog is energetic and easily trained, you may want to give canine freestyle a shot. Check out the Canine Freestyle Federation and the World Canine Freestyle Organization for more information (see the Resources section).

- When tossing a toy for your dog to fetch, make sure it's buoyant and is going to stay that way.
- Bring fresh, clean water, and try to prevent your dog from drinking stagnant or dirty water.
- Only let your dog swim where it's safe, safe, safe! Avoid places where there are undertows and strong currents as well as places where there are a lot of boats and jet skis zipping around.

Dog Sports

Organized dog sports are great fun for both dog and owner, and they give your dog exercise and discipline. (Before you begin training for a sport, be sure your dog has mastered the basic obedience cues.) Search online for dog sports in your area; you're bound to find a club nearby. Listed below are some popular dog sports.

Agility: Jumping, weaving, flying through tunnels, they are all part of the sport of agility (*opposite page*). This sport requires stamina, good training skills, and a highly motivated dog. Your dog can compete in agility trials for titles or get involved just for fun. Any breed can participate in agility. Although tiny dogs with stubby legs may be at a disadvantage, dogs are divided into competition groups based on size. The goal is to complete the obstacle course flawlessly and be the fastest to do so.

Dock jumping: Athletic dogs who love water and retrieving games may enjoy the sport of dock jumping (*right*). There are two types of dock jumping: Ultimate Air (distance jumping) and Ultimate Vertical. In Ultimate Air, the

owner launches a toy into the water, and the dog takes a flying leap after it from a platform or dock. The goal is for the dog to jump as far as possible. Ultimate Vertical follows a similar process, but the goal is to jump as high as possible. When done just for fun, dock jumping is a great training tool and provides the dog with a lot of exercise.

Flyball: This sport is essentially a relay race for dogs. Here's how it works: Teams of four dogs race each other to complete a heat, which consists of a dog running and leaping over four hurdles, releasing a tennis ball, and then bringing the ball back over the hurdles to the handler. Then the next dog is released, and so on, until all four dogs have completed the race. The height of the hurdles is based on the shortest dog in the team. This sport is great for athletic, ball-motivated dogs, but any dog can compete.

Lure coursing: Sighthounds were bred to chase game, but where is the urban sighthound going to find a rabbit? Enter the sport of lure coursing. Although the dogs don't chase rabbits, they do chase an artificial lure. The fastest hound wins! Good news—you don't have to train your sighthound extensively to participate in this sport. Your dog simply has to be well socialized around other dogs and people, have mastered basic obedience cues, and be in prime athletic shape. Of course, practice doesn't hurt either. Lure coursing competitions are limited to sighthounds, but all-breed lure coursing clubs do exist, so if your dog (whatever his breed) likes to play chasing games, you may want to find a club.

This athletic canine leaps exuberantly over flyball hurdles. If healthy, a dog of almost any breed can participate in sports.

7"

Enriched Dog, HAPPY DOG

Take the time to find out what activities keep your dog happy, and you will both reap the rewards. Try a variety of activities from each category, and apply them regularly to your dog's daily life. Not only will these activities keep him entertained, fit, and out of trouble, but they may also add years to his life. A happy dog is a healthy dog, and a healthy dog has a happy owner. Enrichment gives your dog the opportunity to grow, and it will strengthen the relationship between the two of you more than you can imagine.

About the Author

Nikki Moustaki, freelance writer and animal trainer, has published almost forty books, primarily on the care and training of pets. She hosts two pet-related shows in Miami Beach, Florida, and hosted the NBC/MSN online show *The Celebrity Pet Dish*. Nikki's Web site, The Pet Postcard Project (www.petpostcardproject.com), raises awareness, food, and funds for shelter animals. She splits her time between New York City and Miami Beach with her two rescued Schnauzers, Pepper and Ozzie; one pound-puppy Schnoodle, Pearl; and three parrots. You can reach Nikki at www.nikkimoustaki.com.

Resources

General Organizations

The American Kennel Club: www.akc.org

United Kennel Club: www.ukcdogs.com

Magazines and Books

DOG FANCY magazine: www.dogchannel.com

Dog World magazine: www.dogchannel.com

BowTie Press (books on all things canine):
    www.bowtiepress.com

Sports Organizations

American Sighthound Field Association: www.asfa.org

Canine Freestyle Federation: www.canine-freestyle.org

Dock Dogs: www.dockdogs.com

Flyball Dogs: flyballdogs.com

Hike with Your Dog: www.hikewithyourdog.com

North American Flyball Association: www.flyball.org

Splash Dogs: www.splashdogs.com

United States Dog Agility Association: www.usdaa.com

World Canine Freestyle Organization:
    www.worldcaninefreestyle.org